For Lola, Ellis and Eira.

EGMONT
We bring stories to life

First published in Great Britain 2017
by Egmont UK Limited,
The Yellow Building, 1 Nicholas Road, London W11 4AN
www.egmont.co.uk

Text copyright © Egmont UK Limited 2017
Illustrations copyright © Lo Cole 2017

The illustrator hereby asserts his moral rights.

ISBN 978 1 4052 8631 2

A CIP catalogue record for this title is available from the British Library

Hide
and
Spot
Zoo on the Move

Zookeeper Geoffrey loves his animals.
But sometimes Geoffrey is a bit forgetful.

One morning, he arrives at the zoo as usual,
but notices it is very quiet.

WAIT! Is that a monkey out of her enclosure?
And why are the penguins parading down the street?

Did Geoffrey forget to lock up the zoo last night?

Oh no! There's a
ZOO ON THE MOVE!

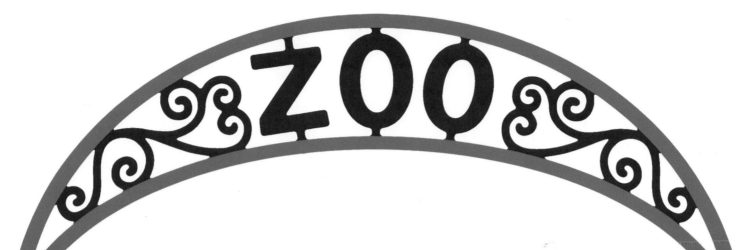

Geoffrey needs your help!

He thinks some of the animals should be easy to spot,
but some are better at hiding than others . . .

Follow the instructions at the bottom of each scene
and use the **red lens** to find the escaped animals.

What a busy road. It's a real traffic jam!

Geoffrey knows **5 hippos** are hiding somewhere around here. Can you spot them all?

If you use the red lens, you will also be able to find . . .

 7 meerkats 2 crocodiles 5 bears

 2 lions 6 monkeys 2 giraffes

On a building site round the corner, Geoffrey can see his animals driving trucks and diggers!

Can you find **8 kangaroos** and **2 joeys** hopping around?

If you use the red lens, you will also be able to find . . .

 5 leopards

 5 parrots

 2 porcupines

 3 elephants

 3 lizards

 1 skunk

Oh no! Down on the farm, Geoffrey's crocodiles have got mixed up with the farm animals!

He knows **9 crocodiles** are hiding here. Can you see them?

If you use the red lens, you will also be able to find . . .

 4 cows   9 ducks   1 horse

 12 sheep   5 goats   6 chickens

It's chaos at the railway station. Geoffrey's elephants are riding on the trains!

Can you help Geoffrey round up **11 elephants** quickly?

If you use the red lens, you will also be able to find . . .

 3 antelopes   8 anteaters   3 bushbabies

 6 gorillas   7 moose   6 grasshoppers

Can you believe it? The cheeky zoo animals are trying to cross the ocean on these ships and boats!

Can you help Geoffrey catch **8 polar bears**?

If you use the red lens, you will also be able to find . . .

 9 walruses

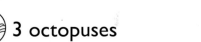 **3 octopuses**

 7 seahorses

 9 crabs

 5 prawns

 2 jellyfish

Deep below the ocean waves, some of the zoo animals are swimming around these submarines and playing inside them!

Can you spot **12 turtles** hiding from Geoffrey?

If you use the red lens, you will also be able to find . . .

 4 pufferfish

 6 lobsters

 14 puffins

 3 eels

 4 whales

 2 angler fish

Geoffrey's animals are having a great time whizzing round the racing track.

Can you help Geoffrey and stop **8 tigers**?

If you use the red lens, you will also be able to find . . .

 6 armadillos   6 baboons   11 snails

 8 toucans   2 zebras   8 hummingbirds

High above the rooftops, Geoffrey's monkeys are enjoying the view.

Can you spot the **12 monkeys** and help Geoffrey get them back to the zoo?

If you use the red lens, you will also be able to find . . .

 4 aardvarks

 4 koala bears

 6 sloths

 8 ostriches

 5 wildebeest

 7 camels

Wow! The last naughty animals to round up have managed to blast off into space!

Can you find Geoffrey's **9 penguins** here?

If you use the red lens, you will also be able to find . . .

 4 owls   2 snakes   5 spiders

 5 frogs   5 birds   5 rhinos

Hooray! You've helped find all the zoo animals.
Geoffrey's tired but happy. Time for a nap.

He's put the keys safely in his pocket.

Or has he? . . .